Intentional Motherhood: Who Said It Would Be Easy

Monique Russell

Clear Communication Solutions

Atlanta

DEDICATION

Dear beautiful Intentional Mother,

There is so much I want to share and teach you about my experiences as a mom, wife, and communications expert. I wrote this book because I have so much to share with the many women, men, and families that I have encountered in my life.

I want to see our families heal. I want to see our families develop tools that can be used to enhance relationships and their lives.

Too many of us suffer unnecessarily because societal pressures and expectations drive us. We allow our culture to define us, and when we do not meet those standards and expectations, we suffer alone, often in silence, feeling ashamed that we either did not live up to what was expected or that it was something we were not good enough to achieve.

I am writing this book because I want mothers everywhere to know that you are not your past, you are not your culture, you are not your childhood, you are not your job, your title, or your status, you are not your heritage; you are who you intentionally choose to be.

I want you to know that when you see yourself through the eyes of God with love; shame, blame, judgment, and shackles fall away.

Through my stories, I intend for you to be inspired and encouraged to develop and express the best version of yourself without fear or guilt. You do not have to fit neatly in a box. There is no "one-size-fits-all." There is only a one-size-fits-YOU.

Your journey never stops. However, striving to be better and better each day is the goal.

With love,
Monique

ACKNOWLEDGMENTS

I would like to thank God, my husband, my children, and my parents for helping me develop into the woman I am today. Without them and many others, this book would not be a reality. Special thanks go to all my coaches, therapists, and countless mentors for your unwavering support. Dr. Deborah Johnson-Blake, you are an incredible woman, and your continuous encouragement means so much to me. My husband, Ernesto, I am grateful to share this life with you. Peta-Gaye, everyone needs a friend in their life who gets them and is ready for whatever. Thank you. To my grandmothers, Modupe Ogundele and Adina Martin, I am beyond thankful for the time we spent together and to learn more about you. I write this book not only for you and to empower the women in our families and generation line, but for women worldwide. I love you.

CONTENTS

Chapter 1

Who Said It Would Be Easy?

I must have been 5 or 6 years old when I first demonstrated my love for teaching. I used to have school with my favorite beautiful black doll, Vanessa, my bunny Wooly and another student I could never remember the name.

I remember punishing Vanessa. She would get spanked and get the belt all the time because she talked too much. She just would not stop talking in class, and so she needed to be punished. Where did I learn this? I was only 5 years old. This memory would be one of many that were later recalled as I explored my childhood in an attempt to give meaning and understanding into how I parent and why.

Many people will tell you there is no right way to parent. Nevertheless, there is a right and wrong way to communicate and connect with others, including our children, effectively. The truth is, many of us just were not raised with the tools to communicate effectively. Without those tools, we risk leaving ourselves vulnerable to passing on ineffective communication styles to our kids.

The good news is that it does not matter what tools you did or did not have. With intention, you can acquire and decide to implement new tools. You can trust yourself and strengthen your inner wisdom with the processes and tools in this book. It will help you interrupt unhealthy patterns and reinforce positive ones if you choose to apply and implement what you learn. The choice is and always will be yours.

6 Lessons Motherhood Taught Me

1. **Being a mother is a gift**. It will not always feel like you are doing it right but allow yourself to make mistakes with compassion.

2. **The best thing you can do is learn about yourself, develop your self-awareness and work on healing your wounds and traumas**. Traumas stay in the body, and you cannot see them, but you can feel them, and so can your children. When you make sense of your own life and refuse to avoid pushing the painful parts in the shadow, you can offer your children similar experiences of **how to process their emotions as well.**

   I was 8 years old when I first met my biological father. He was an African man from Nigeria. Moreover, I was so very excited to meet him. I already had it planned in my mind how it was going to go. As I sat in my cousin's house near the front window, I watched and waited and watched and waited, and with each passing car, my heart fluttered.

Finally, a blue car pulled up. I watched through the window. I saw his feet first and the black shoes without socks. He was wearing this African print looking shirt, and he had this beard down his face, and as he walked up the driveway, my heart sank with each step. I was like, "please God, do not let that be my dad." I was young. Nobody told me to feel this way, but I had the belief that my dad was AFRICAN! I was embarrassed.

This encounter was not going as I had planned. No swinging around and picking me up. There was a simple, nice greeting. We went out to eat, and I listened as he spoke. His accent was thick. I do not remember that much. He went back to Atlanta, and I went back to The Bahamas with my mom. We continued to talk over the phone every so often until I was old enough to start visiting on my own a few years later, around 12 years old.

*Our relationship journey to connection was slow and gradual, and it was not until I was in my 30s that we made true headway in that area. I will tell you more about that later in this book, but what I learned was that **while the father-daughter relationship is important in a child's life, you can still achieve wholeness without having that connection in your early years.***

3

I had preconceived notions of what a father should do, be, and how he should behave. When those expectations were not met, I was disappointed. In fact, I was disappointed for years because he did not show up in the manner I had expected. I also had an idea of how he should look and was already uncomfortable with how he chose to express himself.

3. **Do not worry about what society thinks of the methods you use for you and your kids**. You can change your legacy by using these steps as guidelines.

4. **Practice the art of letting go and truly loving yourself.** The more you love yourself, the easier it will be to truly love your kids.

5. **Mothers have an emotional connection to the heart.** You can do damage easily, so you must be intentional to minimize it.

6. **See this as a journey of learning**.

There are four main steps I discuss to being an Intentional Mother. We will cover those steps throughout the book.

1. Review your life decisions and indecisions for patterns.

2. Learn everything you can about yourself and your history.

3. Decide for yourself what you want to keep.

4. Implement a plan to sustain your new goals.

CHAPTER 2

IT'S NOT ABOUT AGE; IT'S ABOUT

IDENTITY

Age is not the deciding factor for when you should have a kid; mindset is.

I never saw myself being limited as a teenage mom or having a barrier because of it. For years, I hesitated to share my story because of the perceived disadvantages it would bring in professional relationships.

I have often been told that I should share my story with all the negative labels because people could connect to it. For some reason, I could never get with the aspect of sharing an angle that I did not fully support. I was quite happy as an independent teenage mother.

Furthermore, though some family members attempted to stigmatize me, I remained firm in my belief that age was not an indicator of my success as a mother.

When I say it is not about age, many of us have been conditioned to believe that age on its own equates to maturity. Perhaps we can assume physical maturity, but certainly not emotional, mental, or spiritual. I have supported and coached enough adults in their older years to see firsthand that this is not the case. No matter how hard one tries to have this mindset fit into life, it simply is not true.

It is not about age; it is about identity.

When I was pregnant with my first son Jahbari, I was 18 years old. It was unplanned, and I was unprepared. Two years later, I was asked to give advice on parenting to women who were thinking of having children while being in school. I was asked to share my stories and experiences on what it was like going to school, holding a job with a team of 5, and raising my son independently.

I had no idea that when I got pregnant, people thought it would be the end of me. They thought that I would not finish college and my life would be doomed. It never occurred to me that I would not complete or pursue my dreams because I had a child. Why on earth would anyone think that?

This was when I realized how important it is to be grounded in the mindset you have for yourself and your life because others around you will try to implement their mindset of lack and limitation if you allow it. I did not. I could not accept or tolerate any other form of thinking of me not finishing my college studies simply because I had a child!

I was able to spend time with him every day. He attended a high-quality child care center while I went to class, and he came with me to evening events and functions. He became known around the campus so much that he was asked to be on the cover of one of the department's magazines. At the time, I had no idea that it was something to be ashamed of, or afraid to acknowledge. I boldly told classmates and professors if I could not make a meeting time frame because I needed to get my son.

Around the same time that I had my child, another one of my college colleagues, had a son. She attended classes and was the first in her family to actually get a college degree. I observed that the same interest, devotion, exposure, and time I put into my child, she did for hers.

Despite what society said would happen to me, or her, it did not. She was the first in her family to break many stereotypes, and I broke many as well. We never saw ourselves as victims of our circumstances, and that is how I realized that **your mindset is the driving force for everything you believe. Age is not a symbol of maturity or wisdom. Nor is it a symbol of naiveté or stupidity.**

It was not because I was a teenage mother that I was not mature enough or ready to handle parenting responsibilities. While it was not planned, I found myself in a situation that required me to raise my child in ways that women twice my age could not.

It has been said that you should wait to have a child when you are over a certain age, and then you will have the acquired wisdom, knowledge, and ability to truly mother the child. When I hear things like this, I ask, how do you explain middle-aged mothers who lack the awareness, wisdom, knowledge, and ability to communicate and connect with their children effectively? It is not because of age. It is because of their mindset and choices.

How do you develop the mindset?

Early childhood experiences shape our mindset, but you can also intentionally shape your mindset by what you choose to expose yourself to as you develop. Before you select exposures, explore what you currently believe.

- First, examine your environment and the beliefs you believe to be true about motherhood. Society tells you it can be a hindrance, but it does not have to be if you do not let it become one.

Becoming a mom inspired me. I did not feel paralyzed or limited by becoming a mom. I got a job on campus that I loved. I was leading people. I facilitated focus groups and became the editor in chief for the newsletter that was going out to all the alumni.

I found the best daycare for him where students were studying early childhood education and wanted to become teachers. Their eager interest and excitement to be around babies created the perfect wholesome loving and supportive environment for my son. He was one of two black babies in the center at that time. I could not afford the full cost, so I went to social services and applied for government assistance.

My caseworker was a man by the name of Earl. I told Earl I was going to school, and he told me I needed to have 30 hours of qualified activity to receive the funding. Earl initially saw me as someone who did not have intentions and ambition. I shared with him my college school schedule. He said the school was not an approved activity and that I needed to quit, get a job at McDonald's of 30 hours or more, and they would approve the childcare assistance. I asked him if he wanted me to use the support forever or temporarily. I told him it was dumb and stupid to have someone quit school who had a higher promise of independence than working at McDonald's would. It did not make sense to me why getting a college education would not be an approved activity. After a very honest conversation, he spoke with his supervisors. Then, after what seemed like hours, he returned and said they would approve my school activity.

In retrospect, if things did not go the way they did, my life story could have been completely different. It would have been very hard without that type of support.

- **Examine your current mindset**. Explore what labels and stigmas have been attached to you. Have you accepted the label and stigma of society? How has that shaped the way you approach decisions? For me, the labels were: single mom, teenage mother, out of wedlock mom, welfare mom, and I chose not to adopt any one of them as part of my identity in a negative way.

- **Next, examine your current exposures**. Is there anyone you can point to who is living life in a way opposite to the stigmas you believe? Is your media intake supporting and reinforcing the stigmas, or is it providing alternative ways of living and "being?" It becomes easier to effect change when we see a goal we want to achieve has been done by someone else.

I will never forget one of the older students on campus who approached me shortly before my undergraduate graduation. She was in her mid-30s and had a late start in her college journey. She said she was watching me attend school, work, and raise my son and that it was because of me she had options. She did not have to wait until she completed college in another five years to have the children she wanted to have now. There is never a perfect time to have a child. The time will never be the right time, and while my timing was not planned, I would not go back and change anything about it.

When I have had these conversations with other moms, I am often met with an unwavering belief in the status quo. Then, I am bombarded with questions about what my views are on teenage motherhood and marriage. Here is my response. I will not encourage a teenage girl to become pregnant because she may not be ready. However, if a teenage girl becomes pregnant the way I did, outside of wedlock, and has the mindset and ability to parent her child, I will support her in her journey. If the teenage mother has a supportive and loving environment, her intentionality and impact can be far greater than a middle-aged woman who lacks a supportive community and the mindset to honor her own identity.

I respect and honor the institution of marriage but not when it is done out of obligation, fear, or guilt. In these contexts, the behaviors and practice of effective communication cannot thrive because the foundation is emotionally unstable.

Some of my ancestors had children at an early age. I believe they knew something we did not. When you have a child, you begin to discover more about who you are as a woman. Your life experiences are what give you character, wisdom, and resilience. You cannot buy those from a store and put them on your debit card. When you are an intentional mother, you **learn the conditions and behaviors to thrive as a mom and an individual, and you learn how to nurture yourself.**

Intentional Motherhood is like nature. It ebbs and flows. It is not limited to a stuck sequence contrary to popular belief. We learn more about who we are while we are in motion.

We develop awareness when we are in action, not stagnation. Things will never be perfect because perfection does not exist, and I do not believe we can ever live a life free from trauma. Trauma is defined as a deeply distressing or disturbing experience. It can be a one-time incident or repeated or complexed with a variety of ongoing and single events. Those who have had what could be seen as the perfect childhood often experience trauma in some form that they need to process and give meaning to.

From Survival to Survival to Stability

This is bigger than economics. This is not just about being able to provide for your child fiscally. This is about intergenerational habits and patterns of effective communication, conflict, and love. **Carving time out for intentional self-awareness is key.**

Coachable Moments:

What do you feel limits you because of your age?

_____

_____

_____

_____

List four things you believe you cannot do because of your age and explore the limitations in your mindset it. Write out the item and why you feel you cannot accomplish it.

_____

_____

_____

_____

When you became a mother, how were you honored, supported, and encouraged?

_____

_____

_____

_____

What was the environment and community like around you?

_____

_____

_____

_____

How do you currently allow your child to discover his or her identity outside of the boundaries of age?

_____

_____

_____

_____

Chapter 3

The Identity of a Mother

When you think of motherhood and mothering, what comes to mind? What meaning do you give the role? Is it reactive or proactive? You see, many women get into the routine of continuing to live their day-to-day lives as mothers without giving this much thought.

We somehow think simply having the child means it will all fall into place, and this is not the case. In the same way, you prepare for a professional certification, degree or leadership role in your business or at work; you must take the same steps to continually prepare and develop yourself for one of the most impactful roles you will ever have in your life.

The skills that we use to be effective mothers are at the center of who we are as women; however, if we do not take the time to explore this in all aspects, we **run the risk of being vulnerable to pass on knowingly or unknowingly**

ineffective ways of connecting and communicating with those we love.

When a woman births into a mother's role, she can mother a child who is not hers biologically. It is her mindset that is the driving force between her connections with the identity of motherhood. An intentional mother can foster completion and love for children even if they are not their own.

I remember meeting my dad's girlfriend for the first time, who was a wonderful person and welcomed me with open arms. In areas where my dad fell short, she filled the gap because they lived together at the time. When I reflect on her intentional acts, she was the one who facilitated the introduction for me to my sister, which resulted in connecting with one of my brothers. My dad connected my sister and me when I was about 15 years old via the telephone. I was so proud to learn I had a sister, but I did not have her number. I could only speak to her on a three-way call with my dad.

Nevertheless, his girlfriend shared the return mailing address on a letter my sister wrote to my dad one day. I was in pen pal heaven! I could not wait to begin writing to her. I took it back to The Bahamas, where I lived, and started a pen pal writing relationship with my sister. She wrote me back, and I eventually went to meet her in Florida. We found out we had another brother, and we were determined to find out who he was. When a cousin of ours came to visit, he helped us with information, and we were off to investigate.

This was just one of the ways I recognize the power of an intentional act from an intentional mother. What about you? Have you had any of these types of experiences in your life?

Think about an intentional mother in your life. What did she intentionally do to positively impact your life?

How is the identity of a mother formed?

Our identities as mothers are formed from the environments we have been exposed to and raised in. I was exposed to many different forms of family types and structures that included various aspects of mothering. They included single mothers, single fathers, and married; separated but living together, grandmothers raising children, widowed mothers, and close family friends as mothers. A woman who identifies as a mother sees herself as a nurturer and developer of others. **In her mind, she is a mother.** She understands that she cannot give what she does not have and has healthy expectations of mothering.

All women do not possess the motherhood identity, though it is easy to assume so. A mother's identity is developed from the relationship she has with others. Birthing into the role of a mother is expansive because cultural and societal views often limit and normalize imposed values, interests, and behaviors for mothers, but **if a woman does not adopt the societal or cultural identity role, there will be internal and external conflict.**

Many research studies discuss how we form our identities as mothers and the impact being a wife and mom has on our identities of ourselves. This identity of a mother tends to supersede all other identities no matter what, and being such a powerful view of ourselves, it is imperative that we **adopt the identity with conscious awareness and not from a place of default behavior.**

This default adoption pattern tends to happen in many professional scenarios as well. For example, you may be a professional new to the field and feel you need to adopt the identity of a leader, professional speaker, artist, attorney, or doctor you admire. You adopt the default behaviors until you realize that you do not have to follow the status quo even within your profession and that there is no "one size fits all." There are some practices and behaviors that will support your identity, but others will not. **In the same way, we must be intentional in the identity we cultivate as mothers.**

Identity is formed out of the habits we practice. They reinforce who we are and what we believe about ourselves. Research on expanding the self and motherhood identity shares that when a woman becomes a mother, she internalizes her ideas about parenting, and the way she sees herself to others is modified. Society says that women should feel only positive feelings about being a mother, but when a mother does not experience this ideal of expectation, she ends up feeling like a failure or feeling guilty as though she is a bad mother.

Let me just say this. No one in their right mind will have only positive feelings about being a mother all the time. No ma'am. After I had my second child, I stayed home for a while. I enjoyed it and felt good giving my son the time he needed, but I felt conflicted after a while. I wanted to do more and accomplish more. I would often tell my friends that if I only had a 6th-grade education like one of my grandmothers did, I probably would be okay not pursuing other aspirations, but because I had been exposed and had personal ambitions, I did not feel fulfilled. I saw myself as **a mother who worked on her professional ambitions.**

The way you see yourself is the biggest aspect of identity

building and shaping, in motherhood.

I remember coaching a young lady who had gone through a divorce, and her daughter stayed with her dad. She struggled tremendously with her identity because she did not know who she was aside from being a mother, and her self-esteem was tied to that primary identity. For her, this meant having her daughter physically live with her and managing all aspects of her life. I shared with her that her identity as a mother did not have to be tied to aspects of doing, but if she could look at aspects of "being", it would help her tremendously as she continued to parent.

We began to explore the ideas and beliefs around what she felt motherhood should be. In this conversation, we extracted many doing behaviors. Motherhood was associated with all the things that she felt she should do, rather than who she could be. For example, she felt if her daughter did not live with her, she was not a good mother. She felt she needed to cook three meals per day for her child. She felt she needed to study with her in order for her to get good grades...all aspects of doing. When we shifted from doing to "being", which was often incredibly challenging, it opened her up to living in the best expression of who she was and supporting her daughter to do the same.

It was no longer about goal setting or things to do, but rather who she could be. This **is birthing into the identity of a mother.** This mental awareness is a small but powerful shift in how you choose to show up as a mom.

For example, I have a friend who loves to cook. She does not feel she has to cook every day (doing) because she is a cook. Her mindset is that she is a foodie and she took on the entire identity of a foodie. What does a foodie do? They cook, they eat, they try new dishes, etc. So, if she misses a day or two, she does not beat herself up because she knows she is a foodie in her mind.

If we take the example of going to the gym to lose weight, we can explore this as something you do. You may feel that you need to do it every day and when it does not happen, you beat yourself up for it. What do you think would happen if you shift in your mind that you are a fitness enthusiast? With this identity of a fitness enthusiast, it opens up the mind and door that if you do not make it to the gym, you can do stretching at home because of the identity you choose to embody.

Similarly, as a mother, I encouraged my client to think about adopting and trying on a new identity. Instead of thinking she had to cook for her daughter to be a good mom or that she had to have her in the same house with her, to consider herself as a mother who cares for the wellbeing of her children. This opened her up to not being attached to the conditional aspects of motherhood.

My intention here is to share these mindset shifts and tools to free you from the personal and societal imposed cages of perfection and guilt because I know what it feels like and want to share with you what I have learned.

Before I chose to homeschool one of my sons, I thought that we had to do traditional school in order for me to be a "good mom." This is what was normal and regular. So, the conflict came when I thought I was not doing what I should do. When I changed my mindset to one of being a mother who supports her children's academic well-being, it opened me up to explore the various ways to educate my child in **the best way he could be supported.**

Now, I will not lie to you; in the beginning, homeschooling felt like world war 87. It was tough. It did not turn out the way I intended. I had it all planned out perfectly, but would you know, kids are not perfect. Likewise, neither are we. I had many tough times. I yelled, screamed, and was frustrated. I would not dare share this with anyone who felt

I was making the biggest mistake of my life by choosing to homeschool. I mean, they would say, I told you so, and who wants to hear that shit when things are tough. I surrounded myself with people who were successful at being committed through the rough spots of homeschooling, and it turned out to be just great. Four years of homeschooling was one of the best decisions I made for my son.

It is not about the doing, but "being." It is about being intentional in the identity and type of mother you want to be.

"Being" sounds like, I am the type of mother who:

- Embraces difficult conversations

- Demonstrates to her children how to speak up for themselves

- Admits when she struggles and asks for help

- Listens to other points of view

Do you see how powerful this shift is in the way you choose to view yourself? When you believe that you are a mother who embraces difficult conversations, you will not insult, yell, and scream when someone disagrees with you. You will not avoid it because that is not who you are.

When you are the type of mother who speaks up for herself, you will not retreat when your spouse or another family member says something hurtful to you. You speak up and allow your children to see you model this behavior. I cannot stress how important this is because many women are unable to do this, and as a result, their children observe what it is like to settle and not communicate effectively.

My mother gave me many tools, but the tool of speaking up in relationships wasn't one of them. She gave me the tools to work hard, be great at what I do, help others, and have an insatiable love for learning. I cannot thank her enough for that. Because of this love of learning, I learned how to speak up for myself through books and learning encounters because I was a people pleaser. I wanted people to like me, and I felt I needed to take the world on my shoulders. I was the one who could come to the rescue. I enjoyed feeling needed, but that was a recipe for conditional self-esteem.

I worked on my mind, learned about my history, and changed my life.

It will not happen overnight.

The identity shift and birthing into motherhood is a process and happens over time. I was fortunate when I had my first child to have an identity of mothering that empowered me rather than hinder me. I was not the teenage mother, welfare mother, or single mother but the type of mother who accomplished her professional goals. I was the type of mother who parented from love. I was the type of mother who provided rich learning experiences. **These mindsets and this identity helped shape how I showed up as a mom.**

When I was asked to speak to women twice my age about parenting and working at 20 years old, I was surprised.

Some of the women had a defeatist mindset, and with that view, they would not be able to parent and achieve their goals without guilt. I was young and very assertive. I spoke firmly on the importance of how you see yourself and not making excuses for your choices. I spoke on the importance of taking personal responsibility and not blaming anyone, parents, boyfriend, husband, Jesus, or the devil. Some people did not receive this message well. They were more committed to their limitations and defeatist mindset.

On the other hand, a handful of women were inspired and took action to pursue their professional goals and motherhood simultaneously. I did not know it then, but I understand now how difficult and challenging it can be to change your mindset and view of yourself. **I now realize how it will be impossible to do this without understanding what we currently believe to be true, why we believe it, and how the historical patterns impact us.**

When I work with women today, it is easier for me to get them to clarity faster because 1). they want to experience lasting and sustainable change, 2). they are committed, and 3). I have over 20 years of learning, teaching, and rich experiences from which to support them.

Sometimes they are afraid, and that is okay. We all have fears, but every mother should have resources in her arsenal that support her and facilitate her thinking to achieve her goals.

Behind every successful mother is a sea of other supportive mothers. (Monique Russell).

There is no need to adopt the mindset that you can do it all alone, or that you do not need any support in this area. Everyone does. Many of the women I work with start off wanting to *be seen as more.* They may start off wanting to be seen as though they are intelligent, a thought leader, a powerful public speaker, and nine times out of 10, they are. They just haven't allowed their mindset to match their achievements. But, when we focus on self-awareness and the journey to BECOME more, it creates the wins and transformational shifts they experience. Many of the women I work with are women like me, **mothers whose professional goals are also a part of their motherhood identity.**

Right about now, you may be feeling as though this sounds like too much to face, or on the contrary, you may be saying, I need this! I want to celebrate you for reading this book and being in this space. This is a win we can celebrate. We start with small wins because **small wins create confidence.** When you take one positive action and repeat it, it compounds positively in your favor. Similarly, if you take one action that is harmful or negative and repeat it, it compounds negatively.

If you are not where you want to be just yet, let us start with what you want to be able to say about yourself as a mother confidently. This is not about shame and blame. Please be gentle with yourself.

Coachable Moments: Complete the sentences below using positive motherhood affirmations.

I am the type of mother who *(embraces difficult conversations)*

_____

_____

I am the type of mother who

_____

_____

I am the type of mother who

_____

_____

I am the type of mother who

_____

_____

I am the type of mother who

_____

_____

I am the type of mother who

_____

_____

CHAPTER 4

WOMAN'S LIKES VS. WOMAN'S LOVES

W e all want the best for our kids. We want them to grow up being people who are kind, caring, and understanding. We want them to be leaders and not followers. We enroll them in programs and expose them to as much as possible because we feel that doing this will help them to be well rounded individuals, but we often fail to put the same energy and effort into our own personal development as a way to develop our own children.

If we only knew how much influence our own personal development has on our kids, I believe we would take the same or a similar approach with the extra-curricular activities to our own development. After all, it is for our children.

I did not realize the importance of this right away. With my first child, I felt my parenting awareness and intention was very high. After all, I was being asked for parenting advice often. I did all the things I thought I should, early bedtimes, healthy, organic foods, reading stories, no violent films or music exposures and much more. I did not have a television in my bedroom because I wanted to demonstrate through example to my son that the bedroom was for sleeping and not watching TV. This was happening all while I was in college and leading a team.

This was what I saw my mom do, and I naturally picked it up, so it wasn't that difficult for me. Then, I learned more parenting skills and strategies from books and television shows.

Can I tell you something? Even with all this awareness and knowledge, when baby number two came around, I was not as diligent. I still practiced the skills of reading, music, positive exposures, and other things. But in terms of my emotions, language, and behavior, it was different. I was more focused on doing rather than "being." At this time, I was living with my husband, and my in-laws. I was in a new environment, newly married and newly mothered for the second time. Other things took priority. I was away from my family.

The emotional responses and coping mechanisms I used were not the best. They were default patterns of fear, anger and loneliness being expressed. As a result, when my youngest son expressed himself in a way that was simply not an obedient response, I did what I knew best. Punish or spank him. He rebelled. The more I punished, the more he rebelled, but this was my way of leading with authority. It was not until years later that **I learned more about myself and how I was parenting from a place of fear, and not love.**

Let me explain. In therapy, I learned that I had a need for control. When that control was threatened especially by my child, I resorted to punishment instead of discipline. I assumed that because of my title as mother that pretty much whatever I said goes. You may be smiling thinking yep. That is how it goes, especially those of us with African or Caribbean backgrounds because this view is normal.

1. But what happens when our children become "good" children simply because they do what they are told?

2. What happens when we condition them to not be able to respond with disagreement to authority and later, they struggle in the workplace to lead effectively?

3. What happens when we punish instead of discipline and in our absence, they are unable to think through their own choices in a positive way because we are not around?

4. What happens when the children become older and they have no connection or true relationship with us as parents because we have not formed and supported the emotional bonds needed as they develop and get older?

5. What happens when they get older and there simply is no connection at all?

I hope these questions do not sound too far-fetched to you because for each one of these questions I can list at least three mothers and fathers who find themselves in this current situation, and I have coached adults who are in their second and third phase of life who are still hoping and waiting for a supportive, loving relationship with their parents. This is where it starts. Little did I know that I had deep seated subconscious responses that influenced the way I parented. This was more evident after my first child.

As I began to explore myself even further with compassion and curiosity, I touched on a nerve about self-love. I loved myself, but did I truly practice self-love? How did this connection to self-love impact my parenting?

First, let me define what I mean when I talk about love. I will use the biblical definition from 1 Corinthians 12: 4 – 8.

"Love is patient, love is kind. It does not envy, it does not boast, it is not proud. It does not dishonor others, it is not self-seeking, it is not easily angered, it keeps no record of wrong. It always protects, always trusts, always hopes, always perseveres."

When my therapist discussed with me the irritation and disappointment I had, we found an exposure and story from childhood that created the feeling of fear. But I love my kids. They love me too, but do we really? This is what I call a like, not a love. There is a difference. When we like someone vs when we love someone, the connection we experience, and responses are different.

Let me explain. When we like a friend, we may hang out and spend time. When we love that friend, we may hang out even if we do not care about the activity the friend enjoys. It is not about doing things with the friend; it is about "being" in their presence. We share true feelings and desires and eliminate envy.

When we like something on social media, it makes us laugh, it is insightful, and we move on. When we love something, we may stop scrolling and comment; we may save the content or share it. We **may reach out and connect or follow the individual or even sign up for their mailing list or program because we want to give more and be more.**

When we like our spouse, we make dinner, buy gifts, and catch up about "work, kids and bills". When we love our spouse, **we share dreams, goals, aspirations, and fears.** We understand our spouse in a way that helps us do the very best for them. We are intimately connected and are friends.

When we like our job, we get what needs to get done to not get fired. We may smile and be cordial. When we love our job, **we are proactive in providing solutions; we spend more time in the presence of others. We feel pride in where we work.**

See the difference between a woman's Likes vs Loves.

I realized through therapy that I was holding myself to such high expectations and that I passed the same expectations on to my kids. I was in LIKE with myself, but not yet in love.

In the biblical passage of Galatians 5: 22, *it says, the fruit of the spirit is love, joy, peace, forbearance, kindness, goodness, faithfulness,* **gentleness, and self-control.**

I was not being gentle with myself and not exercising self-control when I was angered. I was not really taking good care of my body and what entered it. I was not gentle in my thoughts about myself the way I would be with others. I would also let whatever I felt come out of my mouth because it was how I felt in my heart. I think this is what many mothers miss. We feel we get a pass to say and do whatever we want, then all we need to say is sorry and it would be all good. Imagine if someone did that to you? You would not feel good about it or them over time.

I also was not experiencing the joy that I did in my younger years. **These were all indications that I was in that stage of like, not love and it showed up in my marriage and in my parenting as well**.

How can you develop and practice self-love?

Many mothers tell me they love themselves, but I listen to the way they talk about themselves by saying, "I am so stupid", or "If I had better sense", or "my face is so fat" and things like that. Maybe you have said a few of these things as well. It has become so normal to accept self-deprecating language, but it is a clear indication that a woman is in like status. She is still engaged to herself, but not married yet. Women in like status associate love with going to the spa, getting facials, and going on vacations. Those are great examples of likes, not love.

Or maybe you do not say those things, but you may feel:

- as though people are always taking advantage of you

- that nobody understands you

- that people always have ulterior motives that are negative

- you need to tolerate unhealthy friendships or relationships because you want to feel connected and liked

- envious or jealous of other women because they look too good or they seem to have success that you do not have

- you are not good enough to have or do certain things

- your childhood, parents, and those who raised you are responsible for you not making the progress you feel you should already have

- that if you ignore everything from your past, indulge in spending, food, or TV addictions it's not *that* bad

- that you do not need anyone to help you, all you need is Jesus

- that you have given up on relationships and have resolved to be content by yourself, with yourself.

Sound familiar? If it does, do not feel badly. Many women who do not love themselves say they actually do. It is not because they want to be and stay in like status. They just don't know how to move from *Likes to Loves*. They often confuse self-love with external activities, hair, nails, travel, massages etc. Certainly, these things are important but if you feel as though you love the people around you and no one truly loves you back, you will eventually desire to shift the priority from *Likes to Loves*. Many women are walking around with a depleted self-love tank looking just fine and fly while internally struggling with self-esteem, confidence and relinquishing their power to the ego-driven and abusive men in their life. That does not have to be you.

No matter what kind of childhood you have had, everyone has gone through some experiences that they need to reconcile and make sense of in order to move on from it. If you add bigger trauma in the mix, it is even more important to reconcile and heal yourself. Bigger traumas are defined by psychologists as rape, molestation, and physical abuse. I do not know why they call these big traumas and other violence little traumas because the truth in my mind is **the emotional, mental, and psychological ones are just as damaging**.

As human beings, we are built for safety, connection, and relationships. Our **deepest desires are to feel loved, valued, acknowledged, respected, and appreciated.** As social beings, we want to belong and crave external validation.

But the truth is that wanting this from the outside in doesn't free us up to truly love ourselves. When you begin to value and love yourself, the first stamp of approval comes from you. The approval from everyone else is an extra bonus. I have worked with women who have had horrific childhoods, and have been able to emerge brighter and stronger.

The best way for me to explain the difference between a woman's Likes and Loves is to talk about the difference in behaviors when we like ourselves versus when we love ourselves.

- What are signs, language and actions used by a woman who likes herself vs a woman who loves herself?

  From my personal experience, and over 20,000 hours of teaching, speaking, training and coaching, it is instantly evident and apparent when a woman moves from *Likes to Loves* status. A woman who demonstrates self-love is able to:

  1. Set an intention for her life to be free of abuse **and actively work towards that intention**

  2. Resist the need or urge to "fix" other people

  3. Practice saying no in a way that supports and respects the relationship.

     These days women are all over the place talking about "No is a complete sentence". Yes, it is. But guess what, just saying no does not support or strengthen the relationship with other people. It is not what you say but how you say it. Mothers are doing this and then wondering why their relationships are being damaged. Be careful not to jump on feel good bandwagons.

4. Identify her emotions by name. I am talking about emotions beyond, sad, mad, upset, or happy.

Being able to identify if we feel embarrassed, ashamed, frustrated, overjoyed, ecstatic, thrilled etc. goes a long way in being connected to our feelings and being able to identify when they are being triggered.

Women who love themselves become students of themselves.

5. Describe how the beliefs they hold were shaped by their lived experiences.

   If you do not know why you do what you do, then the awareness is limited. How did your early experiences and exposures shape and contribute to how you live your life now? **This is a question women who love themselves are able to fluidly answer.**

6. Trust her intuition and actively develop her spiritual intelligence.

I cannot tell you how many times I have had a hunch or knowing, ignored it and it turned out to be a decision I should not have made. We have this inkling, some people say gut instinct, others say intuition, but it is the aspect of spirituality that we have as human beings. It gives us guidance but sometimes this compass can be off when we have not taken the time to develop it. We overlook and ignore red flags and signs that we feel.

When one of my friends got married, she shared with me that the day before the wedding she saw an interaction that her soon to be husband had with his mom that put her mind in an uneasy state. (Spiritual intelligence kicked in) She ignored it.

Relationship patterns tend to reveal themselves in one form or another. Maybe it is not your spouse, it can be a friend. Pay attention to the relationships and interactions of those around you from multiple angles and make honest assessments. Put on your critical thinking glasses. How does this person treat their parents? How do they treat their siblings? What caused them to fall out? How do they treat those who are vulnerable and in compromised situations? Honor your feelings and trust your instincts.

The challenge is that children are rarely celebrated for honoring their instincts and intuition. They are simply guided into what they should or should not do. **If you want to help your children build this muscle, honor, and celebrate their intuition.** Ask them what they think about a certain situation and allow them to decide. Honor that decision and allow them to see you honor it by taking the action, even if it is not what you would choose.

7. Freely share about her emotions, both joy and pain. Many women tend to only share the joy and withhold the pain. A woman who demonstrates self-love is able to share both. **She is aware that she is not her emotions, but she has emotions that are a part of her human existence**. In other words, there are no parts of her that require or need suppressing.

8. Describe her blind spots.

    Women who do not acknowledge their blind spots and cannot share them are missing critical information about themselves. We all have blind spots. What are yours? How do you know they are blinds spots? Not everyone who gives you feedback is a hater or is out to get you.

    Women who demonstrate self-love are able to identify this and realize the power of it in establishing a healthy and positive self-regard.

9. Describe their natural style of conflict and how they respond.

If you are not getting it already you can see that **women who have deep self-love know more about themselves that anyone else. The more you know about yourself, the better you are at choosing conscious behaviors you would like to impart on your children**. Our children pick up our subconscious behaviors and patterns without any prompting. They will do what you do more than what you say.

I once attended a Thanksgiving holiday dinner and one of the mothers had her two daughters with her. After spending one hour at the dinner table in conversation, the mannerisms of the mom, let us call her Joy were evident. Anytime she did not agree with something she would roll her eyes and make a soft sound like. Ugh! When it was time for dessert, her youngest daughter who must have been about 3 or 4 at the time came in and asked for cake and ice-cream. Her mom said no, not now, and lo and behold, what did her daughter do? She rolled her eyes and made the soft ugh sound and walked away. Joy said, I do not know where she gets that from, probably too much TV.

I could not believe my eyes and ears. How could her mom not be aware that this is something she does, and her daughter actually got it from her? What often seems obvious and apparent to others is not always obvious to us. This is where our blind spots come in.

10. Regularly says no instead of over-extending herself.

I know this behavior is one many mothers and women struggle with in general. There are hundreds of books and many training programs on it as well. This is in the area of setting and enforcing boundaries.

I remember a lady reached out to me who had a deep desire to set and enforce healthy boundaries. She had trouble saying no in almost every area of her life. I wanted to explore an area where she was already practicing this behavior to see if we could identify some patterns. She was not setting boundaries with her children, her husband, her ex-husband, her parents, her boss, or herself. Unfortunately, her needs were outside of what I could support her with. She **had a strong commitment to justifying why she was in this state and there was not much I could do except refer her to a different professional.** I shared several with her but when I followed back up, she had not reached out to a single one.

Having the desire to change is not enough. It must be followed with action.

11. Proactively nurtures the relationships she cares about.

Women who practice self-love have at least two people they feel they can truly trust. They have at least two people they can truly share their deepest fears and darkest desires. As humans this is important for us to feel love and connection. Many women keep it surface level. Even with their best friends. They hold back and are very reserved. Being able to have someone you can completely be yourself with, warts and all, is vital to the feelings of self-love.

When I hear women say they feel lonely and there is no one they can trust, it is because they have not let their guard down and need more time to re-discover themselves. Then, they need to take time to nurture their friendships.

Here is the thing, it is easy to be able to assess a woman's state of love by how she interacts with and treats other people. When we love ourselves, we pour love out in our relationship with other people. It's just that simple.

The good news is that if you have fallen out of love with yourself that can change with intention!

Fall back in love with yourself!

12. Actively uses her gifts.

    The things that help us to feel love about ourselves are making sure that we feel relevant and are adding value. One of these ways is to use your gifts actively. This brings a sense of fulfilment and joy.

13. Understands her style of conflict and does not avoid it.

    One of the things I love about learning about conflict is leading with the identity of being an effective communicator. If we see ourselves as effective communicators, we will not avoid or run away from conflict. In the Bible Jesus's typical response to conflict was not to avoid or ignore. He leaned into it, said what needed to be said, questioned what needed to be questioned and went on about his business.

14. Loves everything about her being, body, voice, hair, nose, and all.

A woman who demonstrates self-love is not on a quest to change the things about her that she feels are not beautiful because everything about her is beautiful. I remember in high school I wanted to have bigger breast. I would wear padded bras and stuff them. I wanted to get implants. Obviously, I did not. I wanted it to be prettier, more voluptuous, etc. then one day, I saw a lady who was flat chested and so confident, I studied her. Then I studied others and over time I was good. The same thing happened with me when I was younger and wanted to have lighter skin. I bleached my skin. The challenge is when we face these issues as mothers; we subconsciously put our insecurities on to our kids.

For example, I worked with a young lady who no matter what, she did not want her son to have a free self-expression. She did not want him to change his hair; she mandated how he would look and really suppressed her son's attempts of self-expression. She suppressed her son so much he rebelled. She tried to get him to see a professional counselor because she thought her son had a mental illness not realizing that it was a normal stage of growth and self-expression. It was a very tense time of stress. And never once did she think she should be the one to talk to someone professionally to see how her own insecurities was snubbing out any semblance of a mother-son relationship she would have with her child.

When we spoke, she realized she learned her leadership/ parenting style from her parents. This was the style she adopted and why she felt as though she would be a failure as a mom if she allowed her child to express himself. Do you see how confusing it must be for our kids to have parents who want them to be leaders but who are unable to demonstrate effective leadership at home? Trying to override your subconscious beliefs and behaviors are not out of reach IF you are aware of them. **But without awareness, it is nearly impossible**.

<u>Women who love themselves are able to allow their children to express, not suppress their emotions because they have experience expressing their own.</u>

If there is one thing you can see from this it's that if it is invisible to you, it can be invisible to those around you. When we do not automatically know all of our beliefs, how they were shaped and formed and why we believe what we do, it is difficult to expect those on the outside to know and read your mind.

Getting from a state of self-like to self-love includes learning about who you are which is self-awareness. Then, putting actions into place to help you cope when triggered, which is self-management. From there, **you will become more**

effective in your relationships with your children, partners and those around you.

When a woman stays in self-like status, she can easily live her life without fatal issues. **But so many women don't want to just like themselves, they want to experience that deep, rich and rewarding aspects of self-love**. When you settle for self-like, you put your children in a position to see you settle and this is something you past down to them.

I know this from first-hand experience, and I can tell you that being exposed and having a love for learning was one of the greatest gifts my mother gave me.

Prior to that I was unaware, and I operated from a place of my own insecurities which allowed me to feel manipulated and abused. I was people pleasing, stuck in a state of perfectionism which I called excellence. There is a border line with perfectionism and excellence. One holds you back and the other pulls you forward. I was afraid of rejection and backlash and I was ashamed of my dependencies in my relationships.

The type of thinking you have been exposed to shapes the norm of your thinking.

Coachable Moments:

Who taught you how to love yourself? Take some time and think about this.

_____

_____

What did they do, specifically?

_____

_____

How did they demonstrate self-love to you?

_____

_____

How did they demonstrate healthy boundaries?

_____

_____

How did they speak up for themselves with family members or friends?

_____

_____

The quality of a mother's example influences a young woman's mind. We subconsciously tend to replay what we see our mother or the adult woman who raised us, do in adult life. **Now that you have begun this awareness journey, keep in mind that there is no self-judgment. This is a process to help your children experience the best version of you. You are being intentional, and I celebrate you for that!** Intentional mothers do not blame others for their choices. They realize that the people who raised them or who were absent from their life, did so with the tools they had; good or bad.

CHAPTER 5

THE WORKING MOTHER

Jumoke was over 40 when her last child, unexpectedly came into the picture. Her three older children were young adults and were able to take care of themselves. It had just been a few years since she got into her stride to fulfill her personal dreams and desires when she found herself pregnant once again. But something strange happened with this pregnancy. It was like it represented a physical and vibrational birthing and release of some of her previous projects that had been on hold for years. Things she wanted to pursue but had put on the back burner because of her role of motherhood suddenly took on new life with this pregnancy. She had a newfound sense of urgency, energy and interest in the projects that were held stagnant for years. She went back to school and launched two successful businesses all while seemingly having less time. Less time, but more focus.

I believe when you have children and are a working mother outside of the home it is easy to inadvertently put your personal aspirations on the shelf.

At the same time, if you had a desire within you to birth, sometimes the act of becoming a mother births the dream within you.

When I had my first child, the conditions were different. I was in school and working, but when I had my second child, a lot of things changed. I stayed home with him for almost a year. During this time, I did what any engaged mother would do. I took him to the park, spent time with him but after a while I found myself missing adult conversations. Shortly after, a desire within me came up and that was the desire to create training programs for corporate companies on communications skills training. I remember it like it was yesterday. I did not have the mindset or identity that I would be an entrepreneur or a business owner. I simply had the idea to help people communicate more effectively at work with training. I came up with a name...Island Communications. I figured since I was from the islands, I had to put the word island in there. It did not go anywhere at the time, but years later, the desire morphed into what we know today as Clear Communication Solutions, LLC –my global communication skills training, coaching, and consulting firm.

Even though you are a mom, and you have a job, don't ever think for a second that you are limited in your pursuing your inner passions or desires. Everything happens in the time it should, and it is never too late. Not every mom wants to be at home tending to her kids and not every mom wants to be in the workplace. But for those that have chosen a path of an external career, it is critical to understand the connections between personal and business conditioning and traumas. They are linked and show up in the ways mothers interact at work.

Let me explain what I mean.

When I was 9 years old, my mom became ill. We were rushed to the hospital and were dropped off at the Rand Memorial Hospital. It was just the two of us. We walked through the door and was sent to a patient stall at the back on the left. My mom went in and the nurse drew the curtain. She told me to sit down outside on the chair across from the room my mom was in. All I remember is that this nurse was angry. My mother was not doing well at the time. I was nervous and scared for my her. She could barely breathe and was moaning and groaning. Right before I sat down on the chair, I heard a thump. I looked at the bottom of the curtain because it did not extend all the way to the floor and I could see that my mom fell to the floor. I jumped to my feet was about to pull back the curtain when I heard the nurse say, GET UP! WHY ARE YOU ON THE FLOOR? Everything in my little 9-year-old body wanted to body slam the nurse and scream in her face for being so insensitive and mean.

The nurse did not attempt to help my mom up, hold her up or anything. She looked at her with disdain and asked her what her problem was. I could hear my mom struggling to answer. She took her time. The nurse got louder and louder and meaner with each question.

What was her problem? Was she not aware of how she was behaving? It was a hospital for goodness sake!

What I realize now is that the face of abuse and power carries with you everywhere you go. That nurse treated my mom like shit. She was angry, and it showed. It was probably the only place where she could exhibit power over the powerless. I thought, what could make a woman be so mean to those in compromised or vulnerable states?

I have learned now, as a coach, trainer, and consultant that **many people use their positions and authority at work to control and feel powerful.**

I realized that when you don't truly care about the job, or feel miserable about yourself, you can try to put on a happy face, but your mindset and true inner state can drive unknowing behaviors that impact you in your life even at work.

This nurse showed up at work and spilled her personal issues onto her patients. It is no different when I hear stories about working mothers who try to limit the progress of their direct reports, withhold information from others even when they see them struggling, or feel entitled to some unwavering obedience because they are in a leadership role.

There is no difference in personal trauma and business trauma.

When mothers in the workplace display micromanaging, dictatorship or perfectionist behaviors, many times it is because that is what they were exposed to. Cycles of abuse are perpetuated everywhere. Identify it when you see it so you can take a decisive, corrective action toward it. Many working mothers carry their cycles of abuse and trauma to their workplaces and have no idea why they behave the way they do.

Be intentional in every area to expand the love that is within you to those around you.

Put yourself in the shoes of those that work with you and ask yourself some honest questions. If I were my work colleagues, would I want to be on a team with me?

If I were in my manager's shoes, would I want to manage me?

If I were in my client's shoes, would I want to be served by me?

Get good and honest with yourself and answer these questions to see the opportunities for growth. This will lead you into the development and enforcement of healthy boundaries within yourself and others not just at home but at work.

You Don't Have to Do It All

A female mentor told me I could have it all. She said you could have and do everything you want at home and work. You may not; however, have them all at the same time. It was a great piece of advice that made me re-define what success looked like for me.

When you are a working mother, no one tells you that you should proactively revisit your definition of success. You simply continue living life as though no major life interruption has happened and expect to get everything done in the same way and fashion as you did before. It doesn't work that way.

Active intention in re-defining success is required. Once you re-define success, begin to build your community and support around you. Then, develop and master the communication skills of delegation, time management, flexibility, self-confidence, negotiation and public speaking. These are absolute musts. **With those skills in your arsenal, you will experience an inner calm as you navigate the world of work.** This is the recipe for developing and strengthening healthy boundaries.

Before I invested in strengthening these skills, I was still thinking of chasing the same dream I had when I pursued my college degree. Let me tell the truth. I had already given up on that dream, but I was looking for opportunities to hold high ranking positions and climb the proverbial ladder as a way to say I made it, I did it, and prove to the world that I was still able to follow the "path to success". Well honey chile, let me tell you something, when I re-assessed my life and what success looked like for me, I realized I would not need to follow **that path to feel fulfilled and happy.** And I see the same thing happen over and over in my practice. This is not to discourage anyone who feels their path is to hold the highest-ranking title, but from what I have observed, many of us hold those ideals but in reality when we peel back the many layers of desire, we land on something that isn't quite the proverbial climb.

Caretakers Have Influence Too

When my mother worked in the hospitality industry, she would often have a house keeper come by in the mornings to help me get ready for school and take care of my younger brother while she went to work. I learned a lot from our housekeeper like work ethic, and discipline. She was a hard worker, and she would make sure that I participated in the house tasks as well, like washing clothes outside in the silver tub in the back yard.

There was a tub with a scrub board for the wash, and a separate bin for the rinse. I was often responsible to assist with the white clothes, probably because the dark clothes were too heavy, like jeans once they were soaked with water.

Each day, I watched, and observed. She had a system to get through the tasks in an efficient and effective manner so that even if she were running late, which sometimes she did, she would be able to get through her tasks with ease.

One day, she ran late, and I had not had breakfast yet. She knew that oatmeal would be the quickest and fastest meal to prepare and get me out of the door on time. This particular day; however, I could not eat the oatmeal. I had eaten it so much that I was stalled off of it. I did not want to eat any more of it. I said I could not eat it and I would just go to school. She told me to eat it or I would not get up from the table. I said I could not. She came over and she forced the spoon into my mouth and made me eat it all.

From that day forward, I did not eat oatmeal again for over 20 years. Despite the fact that she was an overall good, caring, and loving person, that experience left such a negative impression on me.

Under pressure and stress, working mothers do the best they can to provide positive experiences for their children, including carefully selecting the right caretakers. I know this is easier said than done whether you have someone help you in your home, or at a facility. It is important to examine the mindset of the people you choose to leave your children around and be swift in changing your mind if you ever feel like something is off.

Work Life Balance: The Myth and the Lie

Because of the influences of television, sitcoms and Disney fairy tale stories, many working mothers feel immense guilt about not being able do it all. If it is one thing that I would erase it would be this guilt and the feelings of having to be perfect.

The word balance is a myth because it assumes that every aspect of our life will be experienced in equal shares and that everything will get equal priority and attention. This is simply not possible. A professional colleague and Time Management expert Dr. Deborah Johnson-Blake introduced a novel concept to me of work-life integration. This mindset helps us to embrace the reality of the world we live in. With this in mind, when life picks up the pace, the habits we form, and practice will help us be more efficient. Here are some habits I use and recommend.

1. **Integrate your social life** – one of the quickest things to go when life picks up the pace is the time you spend socializing with friends, family, and colleagues. You find yourself unable to attend functions, but you don't have to completely abstain. Schedule social events **in advance on your calendar**. It can be monthly or quarterly so that you still have an opportunity to do things you enjoy. Take a moment right now to schedule 3 to 4 social activities on your calendar.

2. **Build a community** – it takes a village. Places to build community can include your family members, friends, parents at school, gyms, and kids sporting events or your place of worship. When I coach mothers in my groups, one of the most important feedback I hear is how much they value the intimacy and transparency in the community. This community can be essential to helping

you pool resources, create thinking alliances, provide emotional support and professional support and more.

3. **Batch and multi-task activities** – prepare meals in bulk on the weekend to save time during the week. Use your automobile or commute time to catch up on industry news, entertainment news you enjoy, or phone calls. When you are a woman on the move, make audio consumption your best friend. Integrate household chores into family time. Make it fun. Put on your favorite music and have each person assigned to their chore to complete. If one person is done early, move on to help the next person until everything is clean. In your professional work tasks, batch a repeated task together.

4. **Have family dinner** – when things get busy during the week, intentionally schedule a sit-down dinner at the table without electronics with the family. It is not about quantity but quality time and this 30 – 40 minutes will ensure that you have undivided attention to the family. Use this time to catch up on what's going on with everyone or use questions from Table Topics to get your conversations going. As my children got older and college came into the picture, we would have monthly or quarterly virtual conference meetings. Again, remember this is intentional time specifically devoted to connection.

5. **Automate what can be automated** – anything that has to be repeated more than twice can be automated. Automate your grocery shopping and use a food service if you can

afford it. Items that are purchased in bulk like soaps, and non-perishables, have them auto shipped to save you time. Use a family calendar like Gmail calendar. I just LOVE the Gmail calendar. I remember my son asking me to meet up with friends and I said, is it on the calendar?" If it was not on the calendar and it is a last-minute request, I am not able to complete it. This not only helps you with efficient habits, but it helps them too.

Place all home events on the shared calendar to reduce confusion and to keep open communication about who has what going on. Use email management tools like Boomerang to schedule emails off hours or tools within your Outlook email management system. Use prepared responses or compile a list of FAQs to address the most commonly asked questions at work or in your business to save time from repeating yourself or being asked the same thing over and over. Remember, you are a busy working mother and efficiency is key so you can spend more time doing what you love with those you love.

6. **Be proactive** – if you are working on a project for a client, or your manager, do not wait for them to ask for status updates. Integrate a central location for all communications and updates so that the status can be viewed and accessed at any given time without your intervention. Online folders like google or Trello boards can be very helpful for this. The goal is to reduce

interruptions or distractions by preparing a communications system.

7. **Outsource** – if your budget allows, hire a concierge, or personal assistant to help you schedule appointments, perform research, or handle those tasks that just seem to slip through your fingers. Use a cleaning service if laundry is just not your thing. There are many things that can be outsourced. Spending quality time with your family is not one of them.

8. **Say no** – be prepared with scripted language that allows you to quickly express your choice not to take on a new project, commitment, or social engagement. Many people overlook this step and lose a lot of time worrying about what the other person will think or feel, worrying what to say, deciding how to get out of a commitment, talking to friends about what to do etc.

   Have a script that is honest that you can use to express yourself quickly. For example, "I am operating at full capacity and won't be able to take this project on right now. Thank you for the invitation." It is clear, clean, respectful and to the point.

9. **Sleep** – no matter how organized and prepared you are, if you are running on a limited amount of sleep, you will struggle. Fatigue will cause you to miss appointments, feel stressed, overwhelmed, anxious and sad. Whatever you have on your calendar and plate, it is not more

important than making sure you get enough sleep. Too many of us wait until there is a life-threatening moment to take this critical step seriously.

10. **Simplify your life** – get rid of unnecessary and extra clothes, furniture, toys, and clutter. The less clutter you have the less cleaning you have to do, and the less mental space is borrowed. Less is really more. Avoid overscheduling your kids for multiple activities. One at a time is just fine.

11. **Have a family vision** – last but certainly not least, you must do what is best for you and your family. Your family is a business, and you must be intentional about setting ideas and goals about what it means to be a part of your family—not the Joneses family. If simplifying works for you, then do it.

If multiple activities work for your family that is great. Maybe dinner time will not work but breakfast time will. The key in this final point is that without an intentional vision for what you want your family to be and the behaviors you want your family to exhibit; you will find yourself in an endless cycle of comparison, worrying if you are doing it right, or keeping up with what you *should* be doing. In essence, you set it up to fail. No one goes into business or their career to fail, and no one starts a family for it to fail. Remember, you are in control of the decisions and choices you make.

CHAPTER 6

APOLOGIZE TO YOUR KIDS

To hate is an easy lazy thing, but to love takes strength everyone has, but not all are willing to practice. (Rupi Kaur)

W hat does it mean to say I am sorry to your children? I am not talking about the surface level, "I am sorry" that so many parents dish out without any significance or meaning. I mean a true, heart-felt apology followed with supportive behaviors. So many adults are walking around today with hurts, and physical ailments that an honest, open, and transparent apology from their parents could liberate them.

It is a tricky situation because the reins of power from our titles and status as "parent" often make it challenging to truly put ourselves in a situation or status that allows us to humble ourselves. Parenting is one of the biggest areas of self-development and leadership a person can experience. Marriage is another.

Some parents feel if they acknowledge prior hurts, it somehow makes them feel inadequate, inferior, weak and that by apologizing, they somehow have to admit that they did not or could not do their best to raise their kids. If you this is your situation where your parent is reluctant to apologize, I am sorry. The chances of you doing the same thing to your children are actually higher unless you are intentional to avoid these patterns.

To get to the place where you do not feel too much difficulty apologizing to your children, **identify and clarify your beliefs about the role of a parent**. Your parent status is a title, but it does give you a pass to continue to make the same hurtful mistakes over and over with your children.

Let me give you a personal example. One of my children asked me why he had to get his cellphone taken away from him for doing something wrong, but if I did something hurtful to him, all I got to say was sorry. Nothing happened to me. Nothing was taken away from me. My natural instinct reaction was somewhere along of the lines of, "boy, because I am the parent", "because I know what is best for you", "because I am responsible for making sure you develop character and have consequences" and so on. But, because I see myself as an intentional mother, it made me think, and I explored this in my therapy sessions because I really wanted to have a greater, more loving, and connected relationship with my son. I do not want to have a relationship where there is no connection because all I focused on was raising obedient and compliant kids who did whatever I said. That is not something I want. I want to lead respectful children who can speak up, lead, and express themselves when they feel as though they are being treated unfairly. I want to raise children who are not afraid to embrace conflict when it gets hard, and who are not afraid to apologize when they need to. I want to do such a great job with my young men and pray that another mother is doing the same with her daughter so when they get together in a relationship, they can both practice respect, conflict negotiation and healthy communication.

My therapist helped me to explore this using the prompt of what would happen if I "let him have his way". First of all, that language did not rub me the right way. Let him have his way? I said. I could already feel anxious talking about this. He cannot have his way because there needs to be order and structure in this house. I am the parent. He is the child. Period.

She lovingly entertained my responses and asked me, what do you think would happen if you did let him have his way? I thought for a moment before saying, well, it would be chaos, and dictatorship and abuse. He would overdo it. She asked me why did I think that would lead to chaos, and where did I get that thought from? As we continued to explore this view of parenting, I had, I recalled an experience in my childhood.

I remembered vividly when I planned to go out with my friends to an event. I was in high school. I already got approval from my mom. On top of that, I made sure I did EVERYTHING in the house so she would not change her mind, which let me tell you, that could happen at any moment. I made sure all chores were done and the house was spick and span "clean". I turned up the extra niceness because I already paid for the ticket to the event with my friends. About an hour before I was scheduled to go, my mom decided that I would not be going anymore.

I was like, see, not this crap again. I was so mad. I said no. I am done with this yo-yo switching for no reason at the last minute. I did everything I was supposed to do. I am going. And I did.

When I came back that night, I was nervous. My friends dropped me off and waited for me to get inside. I went to the front door. Mom was standing by the front window near the door staring at me. I didn't think my friends could see her, so I pretended to them that I was waiting for her to come to the door. She just stared. Talk about embarrassing.

They shouted, "you know she is standing at the window, right?" I said Oh, and mumbled to her to please let me in. She did not. After some time, standing there I decided I would just go back with my friends and spend the night.

When I turned around, I heard the latch click. She opened the door and I had to make a mad dash to my room because I did not want to get spanked or yelled at. I dashed in and locked the room door. I was scared for most of the night.

My therapist then said, do you see why you feel letting your son have his way is triggering you? YUP. My process was punishment and punishment from a place of fear. I learned that there is a difference between punishment and discipline.

Punishment is about control. Discipline is about empowerment. Punishment is about one-way conversations. Discipline is about education and getting curious to facilitate better decision making. Man was my eyes opened.

It made total sense to me. If all I focused on was punishment, in the absence of punitive behaviors, he would not develop the independent thinking to make better decisions and choices when we were not around. When adult children struggle with making healthy choices in the absence of their parents, I wonder if more discipline rather than punishment would have helped.

So, guess what I did. I had a sit-down talk with my son and explained to him what I learned about myself, and why I responded to him the way I did. I mean how could I model what I hope for him to practice if I do not practice it myself. He said it made sense and it opened up an incredibly deeper bond with my son. That day, I felt as though an emotional block was broken between us. The resistance we had was softened and it was the most beautiful feeling in the world.

When we develop, everyone around us grows. I want to be the best version of myself for my children and I can tell you with confidence, it is never too late.

If you have a child that you feel is rebellious, stubborn, bad, and difficult, it could be that they are resisting some form of abuse that you also experienced and subconsciously display.

You may be thinking abuse is such a strong word. Let us properly define it here. Abuse is *the improper usage or treatment of a thing, often to gain benefit unfairly or improperly (dictionary.com)*. It can come in many forms. Sometimes the unhealthy ways of communicating have been so normalized that we do not see it as abusive.

When I stepped into this awareness about my behaviors, I went into a state of shock. No one wants to realize that they are being abusive to their children. The natural state would be denial or some form of justification like, "this is the way we raise our kids in the islands, in Africa, or as Black parents etc." But **Intentional Mothers don't mind exploring these patterns so they can stop cycles and generational habits for better emotional, physical and psychological futures for their children.**

It is not always easy

The issues we face as adults often have some roots to our childhood experiences and in particular, the experiences we have with our parents.

A lady in my practice was referred to me by her husband. She was in her late 50s and was struggling to make connections at work because of her cultural perspectives and lack of awareness in how to navigate diverse cultures successfully. As I began to coach and consult her, we explored beliefs around leadership, communication styles and how to view engagement at work.

In one session, we were sitting down at the table in my office and suddenly, she held her head down. I wondered if something happened and I said, "Are you okay?" She kept her head down for a moment and let out a deep sigh. As she began to speak, she said, "I now know how to connect with one of my sons. I know how to connect with my son." She repeated the phrase in various ways at least six times and I learned that she had been estranged from one of her adult sons. Her awareness about her perspectives, communication styles and role as a leader at work helped her make the connection to her role as a parent leader. The insight was beyond startling. She made a vow to begin the process, and yes, I say it is a process to make amends and apologize to her son. She thanked me profusely and I was overwhelmed with gratitude that this leader whose early childhood beliefs and career experiences about parenting were steeped in the belief that parents are always right and have the final say had a new way to establish a connection with her son.

What Are They Saying About You?

Take an inventory of your children's complaints. These are often gold mines for us to discover what is troubling. What do they say about you? Is it that you often say you will do something and then choose not to follow-through? Then making empty promises is a practice you are modeling. Could it be that they say you will always say no when they ask for something? Then preventing them from speaking up and asking for what they want is being modeled for them.

Take a moment to write down all the things that come frequently to your mind. I remember being scared to tell my mom all the things I was learning about myself and my truth growing up. I had the first conversation with her, and there was a tint of justification and denial, but then eventually, she embraced what I shared. It was quite liberating.

3 Parenting Patterns of Abuse that Have Been Normalized

Dictatorship - this style of parenting is very strict. This is a do as I say, not as I do type of mentality. There are no collaborative conversations between child and parent. Communication is typically top-down, and one-sided. My client was immersed in this style of parenting. There is an unquestioning obedience from the child and often they can be seen as "good" kids since there is no form of disagreement in expression whatsoever. This style creates struggle when the child is older and has no experience practicing conflict resolution but is expected to function independently at work.

In a relationship, someone who has grown up in a dictatorship style home may have difficulty humbling themselves to those they feel are beneath them in rank or status. This permeates into career roles, and business.

I once had a client who grew up in a dictatorship home. The result permeated so much into adulthood that it was a constant struggle for him to challenge his clients, or stakeholders because of the view he had of authority. These people were in authoritative roles and were not to be challenged.

Micromanagement- this style of parenting is extremely vigilant and often looks for behaviors to correct as opposed to understanding the cause for the behaviors. It is like a hawk constantly looking to engage in corrective behaviors. Very little hovering is done to catch what is done right. This parent believes that their job is to find the errors and correct them first and foremost in order to "prepare" them for the real world. This style often kills motivation because children tend to learn not to ask questions, ask for help or express themselves in a proactive productive way. They perform tasks for task sake and to make their parent happy. This type of parent does not want to lose control or have them to make mistakes, but making mistakes is a great way for them to learn.

In a relationship, someone who had this parenting style may have difficulty allowing others in the home to help with chores and take on more responsibility than necessary. They may come across as nagging and not giving others space to grow. In a career or business setting, this is shown where a leader delegates a task but wants to oversee every detail of the task and receive an update on the task prior to it being done.

Perfectionism - this style of parenting is one that is very common to many. In my opinion and from my coaching expertise, this is one that is the most challenging to correct in adulthood. But I have done it and I can share what I learned. This style of parenting holds the child to very high standards in every area of life. Academics must be all As, recreational life must be always on top, style of dress must fit into the way the parent believes they should look, and God forbid the child wants to wear their hair a different way, this would be the basis of a full-fledged argument or fight. This style of parenting stifles creative expression. As a parent you feel guilty when your child does not succeed in the way you believe they should. You feel you are not doing enough for them and you have great difficulty watching your child do something in a way that you feel is the *wrong* way. This can be as simple as washing the dishes.

I remember watching my son wash the dishes, and he washed it in a way that I did not feel was the correct way. He did get the job done though, but I felt I needed to teach him the "right" way to wash the dishes. It was a source of contention for us until I was able to embrace that he just had a different way of getting the task done.

In relationships, someone with this parenting style may criticize the way their partner eats, dresses, wears their hair, does chores, and raises the kids as they know the "right" way to do things. They often feel as though you should just listen to them and have difficulty letting go of control. Parents leading with perfectionism are highly critical of others and even the slightest error or mistake that is found will be shared.

I had a colleague who shared with me that he had trouble loosening up and expressing himself because in his home, dancing was forbidden and considered evil and sinful. It was something not to be done and even in his mid-50s, he found himself still struggling with this concept at times.

Fortunately, he is aware of his resistance and hesitation to dancing and where it derived.

I have experienced all three types of styles in the communities that raised me, but if I had to pick one, perfectionism would be the number one. I can tell you, getting trained in the science of Communications and having three degrees and half a dozen certifications did not help to enlighten me either. Coaching, and doing a deep dive into myself allowed me to unpack these behaviors. The good news is that with intention and the practices we have discussed in this book, new mindsets, patterns, and beliefs can be integrated for more productive outcomes. Being guided by a skilled professional is key.

Which of the previous parenting styles were you exposed to the most?

These styles are all parenting from fear, and not love. We think these behaviors of dictatorship, micromanagement and perfectionism are because we love our children, but the truth is these are behaviors that are driven by fear. One of the things we know is that our children are born with gifts to express themselves in this world. We get to help them navigate this and serve humanity. When we miss the opportunity to develop ourselves, and lead from love, we miss the opportunity to bless humanity with the gifts within our children.

Let us take Malala Yousafzai for example. Malala is a Pakistani young girl who was recognized as the youngest Nobel Peace Prize laureate because of her fight for equality for girls. She loved school, but when she was just 11 years old, the Taliban banned school for girls and took over many things in society. She chose to speak on the right for girls to learn. When she did this, she became a target and was shot in the head by a gunman because of it. After this attack, her father was afraid and rightfully so. He wanted to protect her and keep her safe. He forbid her to speak. She became depressed until finally her father acknowledged her desire and she became a very vocal activist, and so much more. Can you imagine how her gifts would be stifled and how much humanity would have missed if her father decided to parent from fear and suppress her voice? Parenting from love is not always easy.

What gifts do your children have that may never serve humanity because they are being parented by you?

"Intentional Mothers get role models to help fill competency gaps"

What is your current belief about parenting and leading effectively? Check below what you feel is true or have felt is true.

- ❖ Parenting is hard

- ❖ Teenagers are rebellious

- ❖ I should not have to tell him or her to do x

- ❖ He is a bad kid

- ❖ She is too old for x

- ❖ If I let her do that, she will be having her own way

- ❖ Good boys don't do that

- ❖ Nice girls don't say that

- ❖ Men are no good

- ❖ Children should be seen and not heard

❖ I do not need a book to teach me about parenting

❖ There is no right or wrong way to parent

❖ Your father never did anything for you (to your kids)

❖ Do not promote yourself, let someone else do it for you

Our beliefs and mindset color our world and what we have been exposed to as a child is often what we tend to model to our children. Without putting the family first and being intentional, we tend to use the same shame-based strategies we experienced as children, even if only through words. When this comes from the parent, it tends to instill beliefs that the child is unworthy, and not deserving of unconditional love.

Now, give yourself time. Take a deep breath. We have covered a lot. You cannot expect these mindsets and beliefs that developed over years to be erased overnight. It is never too late to begin the change. With awareness, comes empowerment. You can be empowered to have a meaningful conversation that may bring relief to you and the person you have it with.

Once you know who you are, you don't have to worry anymore. (Nikki Giovanni)

Coachable Moments:

List the characteristics and traits you want your child to take from you into their relationships.

_____

_____

_____

_____

List the characteristics and traits you do not want your child to take from you into their relationships.

_____

_____

_____

_____

For the characteristics you do not want them to take, list three people you would like to emulate in their parenting relationship. What specifically do they do and what qualities do they possess?

_____

_____

_____

_____

CHAPTER 7

THE EGO-FULL FATHER

The seeds of success in every nation on Earth are best planted in women and children. (Joyce Banda)

I met my biological dad at the age of eight years old, and it took us a while to connect. I cannot thank my mom enough for doing connecting me with my dad because I would not have the beautiful relationship I have today with my dad and his side of the family had she not.

Throughout the early years, I had a chance to spend a few summers with my dad and watch him in many different environments in the way he interacted with his siblings, professional colleagues, members of his civic organizations etc. I consider myself blessed to have been able to have these views.

I did not know how integral the relationship with a father was and how it impacts our lives as women and mothers because I was unaware of the ways in which patterns form and impact our lives. I always considered myself to be strong. I learned how to be resilient early in life.

In my childhood, I called my dad on occasion about two to four times a year to help me pay for something for school. Sometimes he did. Unfortunately, in the beginning of our relationships, I primarily saw him as the person to call when I needed money. I remember needing help to pay for a school trip and I called him, and he sent the money via Western Union. I was surprised.

When we talked occasionally, he would often tell me that I was not ready to meet his side of the family because I had not grown up in the Nigerian culture. It was the sense of cultural pride that he made sure I was aware of and that I would not be accepted if my practices were not in line with what was expected. I longed to meet the others. He often talked about how accomplished everyone was. In my mind, I needed to up my game. One of his favorite phrases was, *"we are a family of high achievers"*. I must say this is true.

When I finally got a chance to meet them, I was happy. I learned about the culture and I was surprised to learn his siblings thought he took care of me in every way possible. He did not, and I realized later, he could not. I expected him to be able to show me love by being emotionally present for me, to call and reach out sometimes, or take an interest in what I had going on.

It was baffling to me because I would often see him put others through college and do so much for them. He was a big brother mentor, and it was shocking to anyone to see my dad so involved in the life of others and not be similarly involved in mine or the life of some of my siblings.

Culture over Connection and Common Sense

As a teen mom, I was ostracized for some time because I did not do things the "right" way. When I got married, there was a similar ostracizing because again, I did not do things the "right" way. As a result, I did not receive my father's official blessing. My aunts and uncles followed suit. After all, their eldest brother made his position clear. It was painful to experience at the time.

In later years, one of my aunts apologized to me and told me she would never stay away like she did because of what happened again. This apology was beyond liberating for me because I had a lot of resentment, anger and hurt toward my Dad.

I was upset that the cultural practices took precedence over connection and it was not like I did not try.

Time and Intention Heals

The first time I heard my dad say the words I love you; I was in my 30s. It just was not something he would say, even if you said it to him. Culturally, it is not a common practice.

It was a weekend evening, and as I sat on my bed reading next to my husband, I remembered I needed to ask my dad something. I picked up the cell phone and called him and after we were done, he said I love you. He literally said. I love you. It was so random and unexpected; I was like what in the freaking world is happening!!!!! I was almost paralyzed in disbelief. Something happened in me. I did not even know something needed to happen in me. You know when you do not know what you need and then you get it, and realize that it is just what you need? I turned to my husband and I said in a slow, loud voice, MY...DAD... JUST...SAID... HE... LOVED... ME! It was a big deal. I called my sister and told her. That was the beginning of something great.

If you were like me, the expectations you may have or the blame, resentment, anger, and frustration towards your dad is valid. But, **until you begin to work on healing and forgiveness for yourself in this specific area, it will be a block in your progress and be passed down to your children.**

When I began to work on myself, I began to see my dad differently. I saw him in his human form, not the "god-like" form of perfection many of us expect our dads or fathers to have. We cannot be our best selves and live life and experience the love we deserve and desire by carrying blame, and shame. We just cannot.

We have to learn how to nurture ourselves, re-parent ourselves and have the necessary conversations. We must release, forgive and DECIDE how we want to participate in the relationship they display. It will not be like what we see on TV.

Unrealistic Expectations Block Progress

My father did not know how to love me the way I desired because he did not have the awareness or tools to do so. After learning more about myself, I began to explore and imagine how my dad saw himself with an intention to connect.

What I have learned through years of teaching communication skills and emotional intelligence is that so many of us simply do not have the tools of effective communication and this one area could literally change lives. So many people could heal quicker and faster with acknowledgement in an open, honest conversation. Sometimes we expect parents to be able to have these conversations because of their role and status, but sometimes they are just not aware of what to do or how.

Sibling Rivalry Driven by Parental Ego

I remember one time finding myself so upset and angry with one of my brothers and when I reflected, we actually had never spoken. It was all from second hand conversations I had with one of my parents. Eventually, I would confront this practice and have a healthy conversation for it to stop.

Or, one would talk about the accomplishments of one child to the other in such grand ways to make one child feel inferior to the other. These types of behaviors create unnecessary comparison and animosity or feelings of insecurity among the children. Alternatively, parents have the power and influence to mediate and form connections. But they cannot give what they don't have, so we do not blame or shame them. We acknowledge with compassion. If you find yourself in a similar situation, I want to encourage you to be aware of this so you can be free from blame, shame, unrealistic expectations and guilt.

Love by Proxy

When my dad's girlfriend connected me to my sister, I learned that sometimes a loving member close to the person you are expecting to receive love from can create positive feelings by association. I cannot reflect on these times without thinking about the positive interactions I had with my dad's girlfriend at the time. Some of those feelings of gratitude spilled over to my dad. I saw the same connection of gratitude sharing in my immediate family.

When my eldest son's biological father was not as active in his life, his mother and siblings were. Those actions while they did not come directly from the father, created positive association feelings and I believe this is what it means when we hear the phrase, "it takes a village to raise a child".

Don't be so caught up in your expectations of someone that you fail to miss the sprinkles and rays of light.

Sometimes the love we expect may not come directly from the person, as in the father, but someone close to or affiliated with them may lessen the gap. Notice that. Pay attention to it. Acknowledge that. Celebrate it and practice gratitude. Life does not come dished up the exact way we expect it. This will allow you to be that love and light for someone else you observe that needs it.

Coachable Moments:

Secrecy within a family or lack of honest and transparency is a pattern I observed in my family. Look around yourself and your family. Was this a part of yours too? Are there any members of the family or children within the family who have not been acknowledged or embraced?

_____

_____

_____

_____

What other behavioral patterns do you observe in the male members of your family? Write them below.

_____

_____

_____

_____

What type of family structure is most common in your family?

_____

_____

_____

How do male members in your family facilitate sibling rivalry or togetherness?

_____

_____

_____

Who would you like to emulate and why? This can be within or outside of your family dynamic.

_____

_____

_____

What practices would you like to model and demonstrate for your children?

_____

_____

_____

What do you need to do to begin to model this?

_____

_____

_____

Now that you have examined the patterns, let us talk about what to do if you live with a man who is leading from fear and ego and not love.

1. **The first thing you need to embrace is time and patience**. My dad was so far left in his connection practices with me that I thought there was literally no hope. I put him in a mental separate category and just kept it moving. I do know that when I began to work on myself, I decided that I would participate in the relationship without unrealistic expectations. There is a time for everything under the sun. What we have today is priceless.

2. **Next, is that fathers who lead with ego need their ego appeased.** This may sound counter-productive but hear me out here. You will not be able to get through to a man until those rigid views are met. This is if you have chosen and decided that as an Intentional Mother, you are committed to modeling for your children how to navigate these types of behaviors they will most certainly encounter in their life. My mother prepared me for school and academic life, but she did not have the tools to prepare me to navigate the various types of behaviors I would encounter from the father figure roles in my life. Remember, you cannot change anyone, you can only change yourself.

   This action step in no way means accepting abuse. It is important to remember the identifying behaviors of an Intentional Mother. None of them include accepting abuse. Now that we have that out of the way, let me explain what I mean.

3. Discover the things that make your father feel enhanced and positive in his own self-image. In life, we tend to

connect with people that reinforce our self-image. Sociologist Charles Cooley wrote about how we form our identities. His work, The Looking Glass Self, is the idea that we are either mirrors or windows to someone else's life. Windows help us see new perspectives and learn about other people's experiences that are different from ours. Mirrors on the other hand, help us to see ourselves in others. His work was expanded by Thomas Scheff and explained our need for conformity. So how we feel about ourselves is not something that just grows on the inside of us. It is made up of how we see ourselves reflected in those we see around us. What influences your father's self-image? What interactions and people does he see himself positively reflected in?

There have been lots of dialogues on this concept. You can see a family of attorneys, or doctors, or policemen and wonder if they were all born to be in that industry, but what you may not realize is the exposure significantly influenced the choices and decisions.

Identify what your father appreciates and values as a part of his self-image. If he needs to feel appreciated for example through verbal acknowledgement of his success, then bestow it on him. If he is focused on appearances, help him strengthen those aspects. Be truthful and honest in everything. I am not talking about flattery. Flattery is insincere and excessive praise. It is a turn off and I dislike it when I see people use flattery to attempt to move ahead.

Take a moment right now to identify one positive aspect of your father. I acknowledge this may be hard for you to do if you have a really bad relationship.

Appeasing to the ego driven side of your father focuses on making him feel good about himself, looking good to others, or helping him in any small way. Asking for help is another way to appease the ego. Fathers, especially those who desire to connect but do not know how, feel appreciated when they are asked for help and are able to provide it.

A soft answer turns away wrath, but a harsh word stirs up anger. (Proverbs 15: 1)

Use effective language. If you heard the phrase, *it is not what you say, but how you say it,* that is 100% true. Words have such powerful effects on us and as Intentional Mothers, it is in our best interest to sharpen the **vocabulary of connection** that you use with your father, your husband, or your children.

Let us look at the following examples of how emotions change with different language structures.

How do your feelings change when you read the following words?

Counselor/Therapist/Psychiatrist

You need to/You don't/You are

Can you talk?/Is now a good time?

Learning how to be effective in language as an Intentional Mother is a game changer. Here are some expressions that may help when giving feedback.

Consider/Suggest/Think about

You may not realize this

Questions

Is it possible that/Can you tell me more? /Can you walk me through your thought process?

4. **Expose him to other ways of thinking**. Many of us learn through exposures to others, books, conferences, other people's stories, television and more. Exposure is extremely POTENT and powerful. Being exposed to new ways of "being" and thinking is the reason why I am able to write this book for you today. I do not have to tell you how much I believe in the power of using any and all available tools and assets to facilitate your thinking through coaching or therapy.

When it comes to the father or male in your life that is driven by ego, exposure to other men who have are driven by spirit and have an alternative way of "being" or thinking will impact his subconscious. You can do this is a number of ways.

a. Look at his community or circle of friends. See who has influence positively and engage with them.

b. Share events or opportunities he may enjoy that expose him to new ways of thinking or "being" even if only in the slightest form. Now listen closely, too many women try to sign their fathers or partners up for programs that you know they have no chance in hell of attending. Trust me, I tried that too. Do not feel badly. We both know that shit does not work. Sending books as gifts hoping that he would read it someday is not the key. Do this instead.

c. Share a movie that has an undertone of a new way of "being" or thinking. Media has been effective in shaping and influencing minds for years. No need to reinvent the wheel. Use the tools and resources to help you. Now if you skipped straight to this chapter thinking you will implement these tools to get what you want; I am sorry to disappoint you. This is in concert with the critical step of self-awareness and identity nurturing and developing discussed earlier.

Intentional Mothers have so much influence and power. When my dad married his wife, she came into his life and played a significant role in the exposure he had and ways of "being." For example, prior to her being in his life, we would never receive holiday cards. With her, it became a routine. She would get the card and send it on his behalf. We all knew it was from her because it was so uncommon and out of character for him, but we did not care. He would receive calls and responses from his kids and grandkids and that began to appeal to another aspect of him.

Another practice she began was that any time we visited; she would ensure he gave the children a small monetary parting gift. It became something the kids anticipated and before we knew it, even in her absence, he was gladly participating in this new ritual. This reminded me of a ritual our family chiropractor, Dr. Chandler had with my youngest son.

Any time we visited he would make sure to give him a quarter. That small simple act created a bond and allowed my son to experience an emotional connection beyond getting chiropractic care. It also created a positive association of him coming to the visit. When my son became a teenager, he started taking a quarter to our visits and told Dr. Chandler, it's now his turn to give him a quarter each time he saw him. What an act of manhood. Well at least this was the meaning I gave it.

If you want to go quickly, go alone. If you want to go far, go together. (African Proverb)

My dad's wife was one of the best things that could happen to support our relationship. She is an Intentional Mother. It has not been an overnight fix and perfection does not exist. This is not a single-pronged approach. **It is a multi-pronged approach and without the component of self-development, it will be near impossible to achieve.**

This is also not about "fixing" the big things all at once and expecting some made up level of perfection. This is about acknowledging where you are, and choosing to create an environment of home and family that is safe for our children to exist as they are. This is about making a decision to do small acts every day that make up the bigger and greater good for the humans we are raising. Even as adults, we can still have rebellious spirits toward our parents, and this influences how we parent our children.

When parents are emotionally absent it can be damaging. If it is hard to be authentic and honest with your parent, it will be hard to be authentic and honest with your children and your spouse. And I realize that even when implementing these strategies and techniques, you may still not get the outcome you desire. I also realize that not all women who are mothers have birthed themselves into the role of an Intentional Mother. This is the reality we are faced with.

Coachable Moments:

How do people experience you?

_____

_____

_____

_____

What do you expect from love?

_____

_____

_____

_____

What do you believe should be returned to you for love?

_____

_____

_____

_____

If you did not learn how to love yourself and others from your parents, you can learn. You can learn how to nurture and nourish yourself. You can learn how to mother yourself. **We simply cannot go through our life not knowing or understanding the patterns in our emotional family tree.** Your parents were once children who needed love, connection and healing too. We all need it, crave it, and desire it.

When I was first introduced to therapy, I had an assignment to create a family tree as much as I could. I did. We then talked about each one in the tree, and the behaviors they displayed. I gave meaning to them. We explored the emotions that possibly drove those behaviors. I began to see family members I judged very harshly in a new way for the first time. It helped me to have compassion and see them as human. I set myself free. I chose not to continue to carry on the feelings of inadequacy and fear I observed in my lineage.

What have you learned and what do you realize about the way you show up with your dad? Are you open? What topics do you stick to or avoid?

I consider myself blessed to be able to have people in my life who can help me make sense of and assign positive meaning to the experiences in my life that were challenging for me. Therapy and coaching are the fastest ways I know to maximize an individual's human potential and performance. I love it so much and invest heavily in myself in these areas. If you have not, make sure you take time to do this for yourself. It is one of the greatest gifts you can give to your children. **When you become better, and more self-aware, you can parent more effectively.**

Fathers Experience This Too; Misconceptions about a Father Led by Ego.

1. **They just do not want to connect or have a better life.** This is not true. Very rarely does a man aspire to be ignored, disrespected, or even hated by the people around him including his kids.

2. **They can change but choose not to.** They cannot give what they do not have. It is like trying to get apple juice from grapes. It just does not work that way. But somehow, we still expect them to be able to overcome and surpass their own childhood experiences which may have been traumatic as well. We know this will be incredibly hard for them to do if they are not aware or if they deny it. If they are aware and do not deny, getting them to actively engage with self-discovery and exploration is another challenge. So, what do you do? You do not sit on your hands and do nothing expecting a miracle. **You get to work working on yourself and decide how you want to participate.**

Many men who are driven by ego learned it from somewhere and society re-enforced it. In some places, men feel they are powerful and strong in relation to the subservience of a woman. They have been conditioned with distorted beliefs.

The good news is that we are not victims to our DNA or hereditary influences. We can and have the ability to change and re-wire our DNA. This is especially important for you, Intentional Mother. You may have a long history of abusers, or addicts, or emotionally absent people in your family. You are not out of hope or luck. No. You have the ability to re-wire your DNA.

How may you ask? Through becoming a student of yourself, learning about your history, making active and intentional actions to choose behaviors that align with the desire of the life you want to have and achieve.

Many people tend to justify their limitations and behaviors, and parents who are confronted by their children with the reality of their truths often feel attacked. They feel ashamed and may retaliate on the child. We will talk about necessary conversations in the next chapter. These are essential to the process and journey.

CHAPTER 8

INTENTIONAL CONVERSATIONS

Any conversation can help with healing (Iyanla Vanzant)

There are so many conversations that can facilitate a release for you, but you are afraid to have them. You have made up in your mind that you will either wait for the other party to come to you, or not have the conversation at all. The only person who gets held up in this pattern is you and your children.

Without understanding that you are standing in the way of your own progress, history is bound to repeat itself as unhealthy and ineffective communication patterns will likely repeat itself through generations. As we have covered throughout this book, the more we make sense of our own life; become a student of our patterns, the more freedom we get to experience.

How we communicate with our children influences how they develop. By freeing ourselves of the burdens of the past and present, we can offer our children connected relationships that allow them to thrive. We can help them promote healthier emotional wellbeing.

Most people, if they are honest with themselves have an unresolved conversation or two that needs to happen but have not had it.

Think about the people in your life that you need to have a conversation with and write them down. What would you say to them? Why is this important to you?

No one really thinks about these conversation blocks or challenges as being communication skills issues, but they are. When we are unable to reflect on ourselves and the past, we leave ourselves vulnerable to pass down subconscious patterns that may not be healthy. The ability or inability to embrace conflict is a big one. Communication blockage in one area creates blockages in other areas of our lives. They are both intertwined and related.

Unspoken Rules of Conduct

As a child, I knew when it was okay to share my feelings and when it was not. No one ever said verbally when it was a good time or not. I picked it up through observation.

Usually, it would be best to wait if it were just me and my mom.

Home guidelines are communicated verbally and nonverbally. **Be intentional and vocal about the guidelines you intend for your family openly, frequently and clearly. This gives power to your voice.**

You can do it.

If you have difficulty communicating honestly with your parents, you will find the same pattern showing up in the way you communicate with your children, close friends, business partner, significant other, and manager. You may engage in passive aggressive behaviors and focus on "doing" instead of "being". You may think that the act of doing is enough to address the gap and void of not doing the real heavy work to be honest with yourself and others. **It is important to intentionally set time to embrace difficult conversations.**

In reflecting on the stories of Jesus in the Bible, he never ran away from conflict. He always responded. Avoiding and ignoring is an unhealthy spiritual practice because it leaves one filled with an emotional hole.

The unresolved conflicts often turn inward and cause problems like diabetes, anxiety, and prolonged stress. These are hereditary ailments that pass down through generations, but we only tend to look at the physical and ignore how the emotional and physical ailments are related to each other.

When you set out to have an intentional conversation, let your goal be to learn, share, connect, and release. Avoid trying to manipulate the outcome of the conversation. This is how relationships are built and healing takes place.

It is important to work on your healing while you are having intentional conversations and not do this independent of each other. If you do this without the awareness, you will find yourself stuck in a repeating cycle or pattern in life. You do not deserve that. You deserve so much more. **Your children deserve so much more. Become focused in releasing and healing so that no matter what it takes, you will experience the freedom and joy you deserve.**

Many women have come to me over the years to help them with confidence building, public speaking, and improving their relationships with effective communication skills. I walk them through an intentional process in my Ultimate Speaker's Guide to strengthen their communication skills. Each woman experiences tremendous success because they are ready and willing to do whatever it takes to experience what their heart truly desires. They surrender to the expertise and experiences I have, and trust me to give authentic and direct feedback.

It is important for me to remain open, curious, and non-judgmental. I do not ever know which way a conversation will go because my goal is not to manipulate the outcome. The women experience significant levels of fulfillment and clarity which in turn helps them connect better in business with their clients, and attract the right type of people in their lives. They are able to set and enforce healthy boundaries without feeling guilty and truly show up with confidence from the inside out and not the outside in.

Here are 5 ways of "being" to adopt when you are having an intentional conversation.

- Be curious

- Be open

- Be patient

- Be compassionate

- Be authentic

- Be direct

Most conversations tend to fail because of misunderstandings. You may not feel heard, acknowledged, or understood; however, the more you practice the skill of "being" with yourself, the more you will be able to experience it with others.

Intentional Conversations with your Family

One of the things I love doing with my family is to have a family meeting. The mindset I teach mothers is that **your family is a business, and your business is a family**. To make your business a success, it is important to have a vision, mission, and operating procedures.

In my corporate trainings, I teach Effective Meeting Management. A study, Truth about Meeting Culture, revealed that most meetings fail to meet their goals and objectives. They fail because they do not have an agenda, they can't get people to participate, they can't get people to stay on task or there is no process for making decisions or next steps. As a professional facilitator, I enjoy creating strategies and content to teach professional women and mothers how to be effective in this area.

Get into the practice of having regular family check-ins and make it fun. Everyone will get a chance to practice healthy, open, transparent, and brave dialogue.

When we have family meetings, **my primary goal is for everyone to leave feeling positive about the exchange**. As parents, we do not hold back. We are very transparent because we know we are demonstrating behaviors we want the children to model.

We do not want to have meeting "burnout" because this can impact the effectiveness of the meeting. So, avoid scheduling them too frequently. Start off with one every six weeks, or once a quarter. This type of meeting's sole purpose is to **foster open communication, practice connecting and express celebration.**

To stay on topic, make an agenda. The agenda needs to be visible in a place where everyone can see it. I recommend investing in a stand-up whiteboard where it can be placed in the center of the room. An example agenda can look like this:

- Last Name Family Meeting at the top

- Prayer/Poem/Welcome

- Recital of the Family Vision and Mission Statement

- Set the Intention and Purpose of the Meeting

- Meeting (each person has a 3 – 5 minutes to stand in front of the room or sit and simply share whatever is on their mind or heart. Remind everyone that this is a judgement free and safe zone. The purpose is to simply share. Nothing that is said will be countered, questioned, or criticized.) You MUST honor this for free information to flow.

- After each person has been heard, you can incorporate recognitions. With recognitions, one person is selected at a time. Imagine if you were in a circle, that person would be the one in the center of the circle. Everyone else on the outside shares 1 specific thing they appreciated or liked that the person in the middle did or helped them with in the last two weeks. (If two weeks is hard, start with something you can remember.) This is to be fun.

- Close

These are suggestions. The meeting can be anywhere from 10 to 30 minutes depending on the length you choose and the number of people in your family. This allows each member to share openly and freely without judgement. We typically set aside one hour and a half.

By doing this, you are creating an environment where each member will feel heard, respected, and appreciated. IMPORTANT NOTE: While each person is speaking, everyone who is listening is only allowed to display positive non-verbal communication. This means they can look and give undivided attention with their eyes, nod if something is said they agree with, and or smile. That is it. There should be no distractions allowed. No cell phones, no TVs, or gadgets.

As a trainer and coach, I often like to close my business and speaking training sessions with something that will uplift the spirits. In the same way, the recognitions segment of your family meeting is often the most inspiring and rewarding.

One member of the family is chosen. Let us say Dad. Then each member takes turns telling Dad what they like and admire about him. Dad's ONLY response can be thank you. That is it. This is not a time to ask for examples, provide additional explanations or anything else. The **goal is to provide each member of the family with specific time to receive acknowledgement, acceptance, and recognition from those they love. It gives them great perspectives on what is being noticed and observed and allows the receiver to practice accepting the recognition which leads to building healthy self-esteem.**

Every activity that I share in this book is designed so that you can have loving, prosperous relationships at home and work. Our greatest need is to feel valued and understood. In our daily lives, we often hear a multitude of what we are doing wrong or not doing right. This type of meeting is designed to create balance between the amounts of negative information we receive with positive. This will ensure that your child and family not only keep the line of communication open, but that you establish and provide a healthy balance of emotions at home.

There will be times when you use negative emotions to activate actions but during this particular type of family meeting, the **goal is to prepare your children and in many cases the adults with avenues to receive positive feedback from each other.**

How many times have you heard a child, or a spouse complain that they are taken for granted or that they are not appreciated valued or respected? This exercise will help to reduce these feelings. It will help them get used to receiving words of affirmation from others in their life.

When you get in the regular habit of having family meetings that include a positive experience, it becomes easier to have conversations that are difficult.

Coachable Moments:

Using the information provided above, create a 20 minute or less agenda for your first family meeting. Include the date, and time, along with an introduction, meeting chat and recognitions. Determine how you will close the meeting.

Intentional Conversations with your Mother

Years back, I had a friend, Junie who shared some concerns she was experiencing with her mother. She felt her mother always asked her to do things and of course, she always obliged.

After all, like her, and many Caribbean and African women, we were raised to honor and respect our parents and elders. I think we get this confused sometimes because honor and respect does not mean to not have boundaries.

What she learned and realized was that she could still love, honor, and respect her mother and instill boundaries as well. How did she learn that? She got tired feeling like her time was not being appreciated and valued. She got tired receiving last-minute requests that she felt required her to drop everything to get it done. She simply got tired and that tiredness led her to speak up for herself.

Like Junie, some women have unhealthy relationships with their mothers, but they would never admit it partly because they are not aware. There are blocks that occur that hinder progress in other areas.

Common relationship blocks with mothers:

- The mother is unable to view the daughter as an adult. The adult child reverts to childlike behaviors in the presence of the mother.

- The mother is not truthful or transparent in her dealings with her daughter.

- The mother uses emotional manipulation to guilt the daughter into being a partner to her. This happens in situations where there is no partner, maybe there is divorce or the mother is in an emotionally distant or loveless marriage.

- The mother expects the daughter to purchase whatever she wants just because.

Some of the behaviors that result from these types of blocks are:

- The adult child suffers from overspending and retail therapy

- The adult child suffers from insecurity, envy, and jealousy.

- The adult child suffers from disciplining authoritatively with her children and expects the children to fill her emotional voids.

- The adult child suffers from perfectionism and lack of boundaries at work and home.

Another aspect of parenting that impacts the adult child is the aspect of Parentification. This is when the child grows up and assumes the role of the parent through responsibilities. In the case for the eldest child this is very common as the eldest child is often responsible for taking care of the younger children physically and emotionally.

This creates great leadership and resilience, and it also has some challenges. I am eldest child on my mother's side and what I have observed is that this can also impact the dynamic of sibling relationships later on in life especially if the younger siblings do not do what the eldest believes they should do. As the eldest child, when you become an adult, you may have trouble relaxing and letting go because you were responsible for leading when you were younger.

Now as an adult you need to find ways to re-awaken your inner child.

As I became more aware of myself, I developed a deeper understanding and appreciation for everything I experienced. This may feel painful to you and you may want to avoid it, but I promise you, doing this will be the beginning of self-liberation. We tend to tuck these things away.

During this process, I first became angry and resentful at my mother. After all, she was my primary caregiver. Then, I had compassion. **I needed to have a conversation with her as an adult about what I learned and experienced as a child. I chose to share what was my reality and truth in order to set myself free**. I was nervous and afraid that she would be defensive or dismissive. But eventually she embraced everything I shared, and honored my experiences. I am truly grateful.

I had a wonderful childhood. I traveled to places, engaged in extra-curricular activities and remember so many positive, supportive and loving interactions with my mom and family members. And though I had wonderful experiences, I also had negative ones as well. This is the way life is. We don't get to ignore, dismiss or negate the reality of duality in our lives. It's often the not so visible and vocal aspects that tend to weigh us down and hold us back as mothers. Without giving it a voice and intentionally addressing it, we run the risk of passing on the subconscious, repeated, unhealthy patterns of connection, and communication to our kids.

My mother is one of my biggest cheerleaders. She's there for me when I am down and gives me honest feedback. She has sacrificed so much and worked so hard to give me the life I have today. She gave me a love for learning and because of this; I was empowered to learn how to parent more effectively.

You can do the same thing too.

Telling your children the things you learn about yourself is a way of connection. It can help them become reflective and insightful about things that they have experienced. Without a caring adult to share an emotional understanding, children can feel shame or distress when reflecting on their lives.

Intentional Conversations with your Husband

When you grow everyone around you can grow. My husband told me he learned about finances from Suze Orman, and he remembered all the books and CDs I had around at home and on our long car drives. I had no idea the impact that had on him. I was simply working on myself. We talked a lot about early childhood exposures and I am living proof that watching my mom love learning allowed me to love learning too.

This learning has allowed me to be to be open and vulnerable in conversations with my husband. It allowed me to embrace conflict and not avoid it.

By learning more about myself I was able to share with my husband what I learned and how I learned it. That helped him too.

Intentional Conversations with your Siblings

It is not about biology. It is about intention. **Relationships of love and connection are not about blood relation. They are about care, concern, curiosity, consistency, and courage. Without that present, it does not matter who you are.**

We are not taught to affirm our siblings or practice connection. I have witnessed and experienced many gaps of love and connection among siblings. However, I have also observed the power of an intention conversation and the magic it can do to a relationship. Set aside intentional time to nurture and affirm your siblings.

Coachable Moments:

Who demonstrates courage in conversations in your family?

_____

_____

_____

_____

Who demonstrates curiosity in conversations in your family?

_____

_____

_____

Who demonstrates care in conversations in your family?

_____

_____

_____

_____

Praise for the book

Although not a biological mother myself, I have seen vicariously through the eyes of my friends and relatives who are mothers, that it is 'not an easy road.'

Intentional Motherhood: Who Said It Would Be Easy actually makes it easy to parent in the 21st century. Monique Russell has created a manual to foster the right mindset as a mother.

Being a mother herself, Monique shares her vulnerability about the experience of motherhood and how her mindset from day one created a path for her to win at what is an otherwise daunting task.

Every mother, caregiver and guardian should read this book if their intention is to carry out their role at their optimum.

Heneka Watkis-Porter, CEO, The Entrepreneurial You

Letter from the Author

Hello there Intentional Mother!!

You did it. I can't tell you how proud I am of you for taking this step. This journey is not easy, but with intention it gets better.

Thank you for investing the time and money to strengthen your journey of Intentional Motherhood. I know that if there are tools and resources available to help me be the best I can be for myself and my family, I would also do the same thing.

I hope the content in this book inspired you to take the next small, right step to experiencing your heart's deepest and truest desires. You are amazing. You are an incredible human being responsible for guiding, shaping and intentionally loving the little (and not so little) humans that have been entrusted to you.

Remember, it is not about perfection because that just doesn't exist. Good and better each day is the goal. I would love to hear your feedback on how this book has touched you. Please share a review, tag me on social media, or send me an email at leadership@clearcommunicationsolutions.com.

Much love and continued success to you!
With all the love my heart can hold
Monique

Connect with Me

Let me know how this book impacted you or changed your life. What are you willing to do moving forward.

Visit my website at www.moniquerussell.com and join our newsletter community.

Leave me a review on Google or LinkedIn and share how you will be more Intentional in your mothering.

Spread the word. We need as many women as possible to learn the mindsets and strategies in this book. Encourage them to join the Intentional Motherhood movement.

For speaking engagements and workshops on Intentional Motherhood, in small groups or corporate employee resource groups, email inquiries at leadership@clearcommunicationsolutions.com.

For public speaking support, grab your copy of The Ultimate Speaker's Guide on Amazon.

Monique Russell is the communications expert you want on your team. She teaches women leaders and teams how to have positive and productive relationships at home and work using effective communications tools and strategies.

A powerful and inspirational teacher and trainer, organizations like the Centers for Disease Control, Amazon, Intel, Equifax, Amazon, and the world's busiest airport, Atlanta Hartsfield Jackson International, trust Monique to guide them in implementing communication strategies that foster connection, community, creativity, and courage. You can too.

Monique has 20 years' experience in the science of Communications and leads Clear Communication Solutions – an international firm that focuses on confidently communicating from the inside out. She is the author of the Ultimate Speaker's Guide, K.I.S.S. Your Destiny Fears Goodbye and the book Intentional Motherhood: Who Said it Would Be Easy. She is the host of the Bridge to U Podcast: Understanding and Black Unity.

Her civic involvement includes serving as board advisor for non-profit groups, co-founding a TEDx afterschool club, sponsoring anti-bulling campaigns in the Caribbean, and much more. Monique earned a Bachelor of Science in Broadcast Journalism, two Masters of Science in Public Relations and Advertising and is a certified Life Coach and DiSC trainer. She is married to her wonderful husband Ernesto and two has two sons, Jahbari and Daniel. She loves the beach, traveling, dancing, and eating sushi.

References

"The Truth about Meeting Culture," Mersive, April 2015, p. 4, http://tinyurl.com/pcqy6fs

Scheff, Thomas J. Shame and Conformity: The Deference Emotion System. American Sociological Review. https://www.jstor.org/stable/2095647?seq=1

Made in the USA
Monee, IL
06 April 2021

64075092R00069